CAJUN

CAJUN RECIPES FOR THE ADVENTUROUS COOK

Cajun

CAJUN RECIPES FOR THE ADVENTUROUS COOK

Quantum Books

A QUANTUM BOOK

Published by
Quantum Books Ltd
6 Blundell Street
London N7 9BH

1-86160-189-1

Project Manager: Rebecca Kingsley
Designer: Bruce Low
Editor: Sarah Harris

The material in this publication previously appeared in
Cajun Cooking

QUMCJN
Set in Fritz Quadrata
Reproduced in Singapore by Eray Scan
Printed in Singapore by Star Standard Industries (Pte) Ltd

Contents

INTRODUCTION

The area to the south and west of New Orleans in the United States is Cajun country, home to a distinctive people with an equally distinctive style of cuisine. With its delicious blend of ingredients, spices and sauces, Cajun cooking is today recognised and enjoyed throughout the world.

Cajun history begins with the French colony of Acadia, which in 1775 was driven out of Nova Scotia for refusing to swear allegiance to Britain. The displaced colonists' travels eventually led them to Louisiana, which offered companionship - in the form of other French settlers, together with a rich source of food. The fertile soil and subtropical climate proved ideal conditions for raising vegetables, while the swamps and bayous provided ample hunting and fishing.

Influenced by the rustic cooking of their French forebears, while incorporating many local ingredients and preparation methods, the Cajuns soon developed their own idiosyncratic style of cooking. And as their cuisine evolved, so did their name, for after years of mispronunciation, the Acadians became known by a shortened version - Cajuns.

What gives Cajun cooking its distinctive style and flavour is the potent mixture of sauces, stocks and spices, together with the long cooking time required. This combination allows the ingredients to blend perfectly to create a delicious - and often fiery - dish. Spices play an important part in Cajun cookery, and each recipe contains a carefully chosen selection designed to complement both each other and the main ingredients.

Game birds, fish and chicken all feature heavily in these dishes, but the most famous ingredient must surely be the

crawfish - still one of Louisiana's most commercial catches, and an easily recognisable symbol of Cajun cooking and culture. In fact Cajun tradition has it that it was they who introduced the crayfish into Louisiana - in the form of the lobsters the original settlers brought with them from Acadia, and which had worn down in size during their long journey!

The Cajuns, and their cookery, remained in relative isolation until the mid 1970s, when an interstate highway was constructed that gave access to the very heart of Cajun country. Within a few short years word had spread, and Cajun cuisine began to appear in restaurants across the whole of the United States. Although not a truly traditional dish, blackened fish - cooked quickly at high temperatures - was an instant hit, and still remains a popular dish. Today the spicy influence of Cajun cookery and ingredients can be found in menus world-wide.

Yet in today's health conscious environment, Cajun cookery presents something of a dilemma, relying as it does on the use of cholesterol-rich ingredients, such as butter, oil and cream. The heavy sauces and rich creams are such an integral part of Cajun cuisine that making too many changes runs the risk of altering the dishes beyond recognition. With this in mind, many restaurants today compromise by grilling food instead of deep frying, and using oils and fats sparingly. This cookbook follows the same balanced path, offering reduced fat meals while still retaining the all-important essence of true Cajun cuisine.

Although some of the more exotic ingredients - such as frogs and alligators - of Cajun cookery may not be found in your local supermarket, there are plenty of recipes to choose from which include more standard fare, such as fish, prawns, chicken and pork. Even the legendary crawfish is available in most parts of the world.

Where traditional Cajun ingredients are not available, suitable substitutions can be made. For example ordinary crab meat will suffice instead of soft-shell crabs, and spicy Eastern European sausages can be used if Andouille sausage cannot be found.

Fish and shellfish play an important part in Cajun cookery, and there are certain guidelines it is helpful to follow. When buying fresh oysters, a staple of many major Cajun dishes, always ensure that you choose only those with the shell tightly closed. When the shell is opened, the oyster should be fat, creamy in appearance and surrounded by clear liquid. They should also be covered with a damp - not wet - cloth if you are not using them immediately. Another important safety tip to remember is to always protect your hands when opening an oyster, as a cut from an oyster shell can cause infection, as well as being painful.

Rice is also a staple of Cajun cookery, necessary as it is both to absorb the rich, heavy sauces and to temper the bite of the hot spices. Seasonings include hot peppers - most famously cayenne - and a variety of herbs, such as oregano, basil and parsley. Vegetables are also a main feature, and green peppers, onion and celery in particular are found in most dishes. Other vegetables include sweet potatoes, kidney beans, tomatoes and aubergines, while for thickening dishes, both cornflower and okra are commonly used.

The recipes we have selected include many of the most famous Cajun dishes, combining a variety of traditional spices and sauces which will allow you to experience a full range of traditional Cajun taste sensations.

Chapter One

Sauces and Dressings

Poultry and Game Stock/
Seafood Stock

■

Crawfish Stock/
Roux

■

Mustard Sauce

■

Butter Sauce for Fish

INGREDIENTS

900ml (1½ pts)

1 onion, cut into chunks
1 stalk celery, leaves included, sliced
1 clove garlic, crushed
1 carrot, unpeeled, cut into chunks
1 sprig fresh parsley
5 whole black peppercorns

POULTRY AND GAME STOCK

Put all the ingredients in a large pot. Add 900ml (1½pts) water. Make a mental note of the water level, because you need at least 900ml (1½pts) after it has simmered for several hours. Add another 900ml (1½pts) enough to cover the bones and vegetables by several inches. Bring to the boil. Skim off the foam. Reduce heat and simmer for 4 hours, adding water as required to keep 900ml (1½pts) liquid in the pot.

Strain the stock discarding the bones and vegetables. If you plan to use immediately skim off the fat. Otherwise, cool and refrigerate. Stock should be cooled quickly to avoid spoiling, this can be done by pouring into small containers and immersing in water/ice. After several hours the fat will have congealed and can be removed easily from the top. The stock can then be returned to a fridge or freezer.

SEAFOOD STOCK

Use 900g (2lbs), any combination of prawn shells and heads, crab shells, crayfish heads and shells, lobster carcasses and fish carcasses with heads and gills removed. You may also add oyster liquid. You may also add trimmings from any other vegetable – except green peppers – you are using in a particular recipe.

Method and ingredients – As above.

Crawfish Stock

Add all the ingredients, except the crawfish, to a large stockpot of boiling water and boil for 15-20 minutes to develop the flavour, then add the crawfish. Return to the boil, then simmer for 20 minutes. Remove the crawfish with tongs and plunge into cold water. Return the stock to a low heat to simmer while you clean the crawfish.

To clean the crawfish, twist off the tails from the bodies, and cut out all the tail meat. Save the tail meat in 1 bowl. Remove the yellow fat from the bodies and save the fat in a second bowl. Pull the body shells – the thorax – free from the innards, and break off eyes and beaks. Save the best shells for stuffing. Place the innards, any small or broken shells, the heads and the remains of the tail shells in the stock, and continue simmering for total cooking time of 2 hours.

Strain the stock, discarding the vegetables and shells. Reserve 1.25 1 (2¼ pts) stock: freeze any leftover for future use.

Ingredients

1 large onion, sliced
1 lemon, sliced
2 garlic cloves, crushed
3 fresh parsley sprigs
1 stalk celery, including leaves, sliced
2 whole cloves
15ml (1 tbsp) whole mustard seed
5ml (1 tsp) celery seed
2 bay leaves
2.5 ml (½ tsp) red-pepper flakes
5ml (1tsp) black pepper
5 ml (1 tsp) salt
2.25kg (5 lbs) whole crawfish

Roux

In a heavy saucepan over medium-low to low heat, melt the lard. When it is hot, add about one-third of the flour at a time, whisking it until smooth each time. Continue stirring after all the flour is added. As the roux cooks, you will see the colour darken and it will develop a nutty smell. Continue cooking until the roux reaches the desired colour. DO NOT STOP STIRRING UNTIL THE ROUX IS DONE.

When the roux reaches the desired colour, remove it from the heat and stir in vegetables to stop the cooking. If no vegetables are called for, pour the roux into a metal bowl and continue stirring for 5-10 minutes until the darkening stops. At this point, you may return the roux and vegetables to the stock and continue the recipe, or set the roux aside and let it cool.

Excess roux may be refrigerated or frozen.

Ingredients

225g (8 oz) lard
100g (4oz) plain flour

MUSTARD SAUCE

MAKES ABOUT 300 ML (1/2 PT)

INGREDIENTS

250 ml (8 fl oz) soured cream
45 ml (3 tbsp) Dijon-style mustard
30 ml (2 tbsp) mayonnaise
15 ml (1 tbsp) chopped fresh dill or 5 ml (1 tsp) dry dill weed
fresh-ground black pepper

In a small bowl, whisk all the ingredients together. Chill for several hours to allow the flavours to blend.

BUTTER SAUCE FOR FISH

MAKES 4–6 SERVINGS

INGREDIENTS

1 spring onion, finely chopped
30 ml (2 tbsp) dry white wine
30 ml (2 tbsp) white wine vinegar
50 g (2 oz) butter
60 ml (2 fl oz) double cream
salt
white pepper

In a small saucepan, simmer the onion, wine and vinegar until the liquid is reduced to 15 ml (1 tbsp). Over very low heat, whisk in the butter, 15 ml (1 tbsp) at a time. Whisk in the cream until smooth. Warm, but don't let sauce bubble. Season with salt and pepper to taste.

VARIATION:
Add 15 ml (1 tbsp) chopped fresh dill at the beginning, before the reduction. Add 15 ml (1 tbsp) chopped fresh dill with the salt and pepper.

Chapter Two

Soups and Appetizers

Oysters Rockefeller

■

Cajun Devilled Eggs

■

Crawfish Bisque/
Stuffed Crawfish

■

Oysters Bienville

■

Crab-Corn Chowder

■

Cold Prawns in Horseradish Sauce

■

Cajun BBQ Prawns

■

Crab-stuffed Mushrooms

■

Oyster Stew

■

Hot Crab Spread

Oysters Rockefeller

SERVES 4

Ingredients

rock salt
50 g (2 oz) butter
225 g (8 oz) chopped fresh spinach
45 ml (3 tbsp) chopped fresh parsley
6 spring onions, chopped
30 ml (2 tbsp) finely chopped celery
15 ml (1 tbsp) finely chopped green pepper
1.5 ml (¼ tsp) salt
1.5 ml (¼ tsp aniseed
7.5 ml (1½ tsp) fresh thyme or 2.5 ml (½ tsp) dried
15 ml (1 tbsp) anchovy paste
45 ml (3 tbsp) dry breadcrumbs
120 ml (4 fl oz) double cream
pinch of fresh ground black pepper
few drops of Tabasco sauce
20 oysters on the half shells

Oven Temperature:
200°C/400°F/Gas Mark 6

Pour the rock salt about 1.2 cm/½ inch deep into a large baking pan, and put into the oven at 200°C/400°F/Gas Mark 6. The salt serves to keep the oysters from tipping over, and it will help keep them warm after they come out of the oven.

In a frying pan over low heat, melt the butter. Sauté the spinach, parsley, onions, celery and green pepper until the spinach is thoroughly wilted, about 6 minutes. Add remaining ingredients, except the oysters, stirring in a little extra cream or breadcrumbs as needed to achieve the consistency of a thick sauce.

Put 1 oyster on each half shelf and spoon some of the sauce over each oyster. Nestle the oysters in the heated rock salt. Bake at 200°C/400°F/Gas Mark 6 until the topping is bubbly, about 12 minutes.

CAJUN DEVILLED EGGS

MAKES 6

INGREDIENTS

6 eggs, hard-boiled and shelled
25 g (1 oz) Tasso, finely chopped
15 ml (1 tbsp) finely chopped green pepper
1 spring onion, finely chopped
2.5 ml (½ tsp) fresh-squeezed lemon juice
30 ml (2 tbsp) mayonnaise
30 ml (2 tbsp) Dijon-style mustard
dash of fresh-ground pepper
1–2 drops of Tabasco sauce

Cut the eggs in half lengthways. Remove the yolks and put them in a small bowl and set aside the whites. Mash the yolks with a fork. Add the remaining ingredients to the yolks and mix well with a fork. Taste and adjust the seasonings. Spoon the mixture into the egg whites.

CRAWFISH BISQUE

Make a dark, mahogany-coloured roux of lard and flour (page 13). Remove from heat and stir in the tomato, celery, garlic, onion and green pepper. Return to very low heat and cook until vegetables are limp, about 5 minutes. Set aside.

In a large pot, bring the crawfish stock to the boil. Add the roux and vegetables to the stock 1 spoonful at a time, whisking to mix thoroughly. Add the crawfish tail meat, fat, seasonings and lemon juice. Gently, with tongs or large spoon, add the stuffed shells to soup. Simmer for 45 minutes, uncovered.

Put rice in bottom of each bowl. Fish out the stuffed shells and divide among the bowls. Add the spring onions to the soup, then ladle the bisque into the bowls.

INGREDIENTS

60ml (4 tbsp) plain flour
50g (2 oz) lard
1 medium tomato, seeded and chopped
1 stalk celery, chopped
1 clove garlic, finely chopped
100g (4 oz) onion, chopped
½ green pepper, chopped
1.25l (2¼ pts) reserved crawfish stock (p.13)
½ reserved crawfish tail meat
½ reserved crawfish fat
5 ml (1 tsp) fresh thyme or 1.5ml(¼ tsp x 4) dried
1 bay leaf
5 ml (1 tsp) Worcestershire sauce
½ tsp salt
¼ tsp black pepper
large pinch cayenne
1 tsp fresh-squeezed lemon juice
reserved stuffed crawfish shells (below)
350g (12 oz) cooked rice to serve
100g (4 oz) spring onions, chopped

STUFFED CRAWFISH

Thoroughly clean the crawfish shells, removing any bits of innards that remain. Let dry on kitchen paper.
In a large frying pan, melt the butter over a low heat. sauté the onions, green pepper, celery and garlic, 5 minutes. Remove from the heat, and put in a bowl with the remaining ingredients, except the stock. The stuffing should be moist enough that it sticks together when you roll some into a small ball: it should not be mushy. Add some more stock if needed.

Fill the crawfish shells with cornbread mixture, pressing the stuffing so it is solid and not crumbly. Put the stuffed shells on an ungreased baking sheet at 350°F/Gas mark 4/180°c for 10 minutes. Remove from oven and set aside.

INGREDIENTS

4-5 crawfish bodies per person
25g (1oz) butter
100g (4oz) onion, chopped
½ green pepper, chopped
1 stalk celery, chopped
2 cloves garlic, finely chopped
15ml (1 tbsp) chopped fresh parsley
5ml (1 tsp) fresh tyme or ¼ dried
2.5ml (½ tsp) salt
large pinch black pepper
few drops of tabasco sauce
1 tsp lemon juice
1 egg, lightly beaten
100g (4 oz) finely crumbled cornbread
½ reserved crawfish tail meat, ground or finely chopped
½ reserved crawfish fat
reserved crawfish stock to moisten if required.

Oysters Bienville

SERVES 3–4

Ingredients

rock salt
26 g (1 oz) butter
3 spring onions, chopped
2 cloves garlic, chopped
1 tbsp finely chopped fresh parsley
4 large mushrooms, finely chopped
15 g (½ oz) plain flour
175 ml (6 fl oz) double cream
100 g (4 oz) prawns, shelled, deveined, cooked and finely chopped
1 egg yolk, lightly beaten
15 ml (1 tbsp) dry sherry
large pinch black pepper
large pinch cayenne
5 ml (1 tsp) Worcestershire sauce
pinch of salt
75 ml (5 tbsp) grated Parmesan cheese
30 ml (2 tbsp) dry breadcrumbs
2.5 ml (¼ tsp) salt
16 oysters on the half shell

Oven Temperature:
200°C/400°F/Gas Mark 6

Pour the rock salt about 1.3 cm (½ inch) deep into a large baking tin, or several tins, large enough to hold all the oysters in one layer, and put in oven at 200°C/400°F/Gas Mark 6. The salt keeps the oysters from tipping over, and will help keep them warm after they come out of the oven.

In a frying pan over a moderate heat, melt the butter. Sauté the spring onions, garlic, parsley and mushrooms until the vegetables are limp, about 5 minutes. Add the flour and stir until blended. Add the cream and stir until blended. Add the prawns, egg yolk, sherry, black pepper, cayenne, Worcestershire sauce and salt and cook until the mixture thickens, stirring, 5–6 minutes.

In a small bowl, make the crumb topping mixture. Combine the Parmesan, breadcrumbs, salt, cayenne and pepper.

Put 1 oyster on each half shell and spoon some prawn sauce over each oyster. Top each with the crumb mixture. Nestle the oysters in hot rock salt. Bake at 200°C/400°F/Gas Mark 6 until the topping is golden, 12–15 minutes.

Crab-corn Chowder

SERVES 4

Ingredients

25 g (2 tbsp) butter
½ onion, chopped
1 stalk celery, finely chopped
1 clove garlic, finely chopped
350 ml (2 fl oz) seafood stock (page 12)
120 ml (4 fl oz) dry white wine or poultry stock (page 12)
175 g (6 oz) fresh or frozen corn kernels
1.5 ml (¼ tsp) dried thyme
2.5 ml (½ tsp) salt
dash of cayenne
1.5 ml (¼ tsp) white pepper
250 ml (8 fl oz) single cream
120 ml (4 fl oz) soured cream
100 g (4 oz) crab meat
15 ml (1 tbsp) chopped fresh parsley
2 spring onions, chopped

In a large saucepan over low heat, melt the butter. Sauté the onion, celery and garlic until wilted, about 5 minutes.

Add the seafood stock and wine and bring to the boil. Add the corn and spices. Return to the boil, then reduce the heat and simmer, uncovered, about 20 minutes. Stir in the cream and continue summering for 10 minutes but do not boil. Whisk in the soured cream.

Add the crab meat, parsley and spring onions, and heat just enough to warm the crab. Do not allow to boil.

Cold Prawns in Horseradish Sauce

SERVES 4–6

Ingredients

30 ml (2 tbsp) cider vinegar
30 ml (2 tbsp) lemon juice
45 ml (3 tbsp) olive oil
2 cloves garlic, finely chopped
45 ml (3 tbsp) chopped spring onions
30 ml (2 tbsp) finely chopped fresh parsley
5 ml (1 tsp) red-pepper flakes
5 ml (1 tsp) Creole mustard
30 ml (2 tbsp) Dijon-style mustard
30 ml (2 tbsp) prepared horseradish
2.5 g (½ tsp) celery seed
450 g (1 lb) medium cooked prawns, shelled and deveined

In a bowl, combine all the ingredients, except the prawns, and mix well. Add the prawns making sure each piece is well coated. Refrigerate for at least 3 hours or as long as 24 hours.

INGREDIENTS

350 g (12 oz) unsalted butter
6 garlic cloves, finely chopped
15 ml (1 tbsp) chopped fresh basil or 15 ml (1 tsp) dried
10 ml (2 tsp) fresh rosemary or 2.5 ml (½ tsp) dried
7.5 ml (1½ tsp) fresh oregano or 2.5 ml (½ tsp) dried
250 ml (8 fl oz) seafood stock (page 12)
20 ml (4 tsp) fresh-squeezed lemon juice
15 ml (1 tbsp) Worcestershire sauce
2.5 ml (½ tsp) salt
10 ml (2 tsp) cayenne
5 ml (1 tsp) paprika
10 ml (2 tsp) dry mustard
5 ml (1 tsp) red-pepper flakes
675 g (1½ lbs) medium unshelled prawns

CAJUN BBQ PRAWNS

SERVES 6–8

In a heavy saucepan over low heat, melt the butter, swirling occasionally and taking care that butter does not brown. As soon as the butter starts to melt, add the garlic and herbs, and continue swirling until butter is completely melted.

Add the remaining ingredients, except the prawns, and use a wire whisk to mix well. Simmer over low heat to allow flavours to blend, about 15 minutes. Add the prawns and cook just until prawns are opaque and curled, 5–7 minutes. Remove from heat and pour carefully into a heatproof serving dish.

CRAB-STUFFED MUSHROOMS

MAKES 24

OVEN TEMPERATURE:
180°C/350°F/GAS MARK4

Clean the mushrooms and separate the stems from the caps. Meanwhile, finely chop the stems. Steam the mushrooms for 5 minutes, then set aside.

In a frying pan over medium heat, melt the butter. Add the chopped stems, spring onions and garlic and cook until most of the liquid is evaporated, 8–10 minutes. Add the salt, cayenne, bread-crumbs and cream, and mix well. Gently stir in the crab meat and cook until just heated through.

Stuff the mushroom caps with the crab mixture, mounding a little on each top. Sprinkle each with Parmesan cheese. Arrange on a lightly greased baking sheet. Bake at 180°C/350°F/Gas Mark 6 for 10 minutes, then broil 2–3 minutes until the cheese turns golden brown.

INGREDIENTS

24 large fresh mushrooms
25 g (1 oz) butter
4 spring onions, chopped
1 clove garlic, finely chopped
2.5 ml (½ tsp) salt
1.5 ml (¼ tsp) cayenne
25 g (1 oz) dry breadcrumbs
60 ml (2 fl oz) double cream
350 g (12 oz) fresh crab meat, picked over, or frozen or tinned, well drained
Parmesan cheese

Oyster Stew

SERVES 4

Ingredients

25 g (1 oz) butter
4 spring onions, finely chopped
1 stalk celery, finely chopped
1.1 l (2 pts) single cream
2.5 (½ tsp) salt
1.5 ml (¼ tsp) cayenne
10 ml (2 tsp) Worcestershire sauce
3 dozen large or 4 dozen small-medium oysters with their juice, large oysters halved
butter or sherry for garnishing

In a medium saucepan over low heat, melt the butter. Sauté the spring onions and celery until limp, about 5 minutes.

Add the single cream, salt, cayenne and Worcestershire sauce and heat until the soup just starts to boil. Lower the heat, add the oysters and their liquor, and cook just until the edges of the oysters start to curl, 2–3 minutes. Taste and adjust the seasonings.

You may garnish each bowl with a pat of butter or a dash of sherry, if you like.

Hot Crab Spread

Ingredients

3 tbsp soured cream
75 g (3 oz) cream cheese
15 ml (1 tbsp) fresh-squeezed lemon juice
2.5 ml (½ tsp) prepared horseradish
15 ml (1 tbsp) chopped fresh dill
2 spring onions, finely chopped
dash of salt
dash of freshground black pepper

Oven Temperature:
180°C/350°F/Gas Mark 4

Cream the soured cream and cream cheese together with an electric beater. Add the remaining ingredients, except the crab, and beat until smooth. Gently stir in the crab.

Put the mixture in an ovenproof serving dish and bake at 180°C/350°F/Gas Mark 4 until hot, about 15 minutes.

Chapter Three

Pasta, Rice and Vegetables

Greens and Tasso

■

BBQ Spicy Vegetables and Potatoes

■

Crawfish and Tasso in Cream Sauce Over Fettucine

■

Trinity Rice with Almonds

■

Corn Manque Choux

■

Spicy Green Beans

■

Red Beans and Rice with Tasso and Andouille

■

Duck Rice

■

Deep Fried Aubergine

Greens and Tasso

SERVES 4

Ingredients

2 bunches greens

½ onion, chopped

75 g (3 oz) Tasso, chopped

Wash the greens very thoroughly, until all the sand is removed. This may take 3 or 4 washings. Tear the greens into pieces and chop the stems.

Put the greens into a pot with the onion, Tasso and 1 cup water. Bring to the boil, then cover and reduce the heat and simmer, stirring occasionally, until stems are tender, about 40 minutes. Drain off water and serve.

BARBECUED SPICY VEGETABLES AND POTATOES

Slice red potatoes, courgettes or aubergines about 5mm (¼ in) thick or slightly thicker. Both these vegetables are attractive cut at a diagonal; cut marrow or gourds in half lengthways.

Brush the cut edges lightly with olive oil and sprinkle with your favourite spices – paprika and cumin work well in this recipe, dried herbs do not. Lightly salt the potatoes, if desired.

When the barbecue coals are no longer flaming, place the vegetables on the grill. Turn once during cooking: marrow and courgettes cook quickly, about 5 minutes; aubergines takes 1–2 minutes longer; potatoes take about 10 minutes. Cooking times are a little shorter if the vegetables are directly over the coals instead of around the edges.

INGREDIENTS

sliced vegetables

olive oil

paprika and cumin or other spices

salt

CRAWFISH AND TASSO IN CREAM SAUCE OVER FETTUCINE

SERVES 4

In a large frying pan, melt the butter. Sauté the spring onions and garlic about 2 minutes. Add wine, 60 ml (2 fl oz) seafood stock and the Tasso and cook until slightly bubbly. Reduce the heat and simmer until liquid is reduced slightly, about 10 minutes.

Dissolve the flour in remaining 60 ml (2 fl oz) seafood stock, then add to the sauce and stir until smooth. Stir in the crawfish tails and the single cream. Mix well and heat just until bubbly. Taste and adjust salt. Serve over fettucine.

INGREDIENTS

75 g (3 oz) butter
8–10 spring onions, chopped
3 cloves garlic, finely chopped
120 ml (4 fl oz) dry white wine
120 ml (4 fl oz) seafood stock (page 12) or clam juice
150 g (5 oz) diced Tasso
25 g (1 oz) plain flour
225 g (8 oz) cooked and shelled crawfish tails
475 ml (16 fl oz) single cream
salt to taste
hot cooked fettucine to serve

TRINITY RICE WITH ALMONDS

MAKES 8 SIDE-DISH SERVINGS

INGREDIENTS

25 g (1 oz) butter or olive oil
1 stalk celery, chopped
1 small green pepper, chopped
100 g (4 oz) onion, chopped
2 cloves garlic, finely chopped
75 g (3 oz) blanched almonds, slivered or sliced
5 ml (1 tsp) Worcestershire sauce
7.5 ml (1½ tsp) salt
1.5 ml (¼ tsp) black pepper
1 tomato, seeded and chopped
4–5 spring onions, chopped
30 ml (2 tbsp) chopped fresh parsley
225 g (8 oz) white rice

In a medium frying pan, heat the butter or olive oil. Sauté the celery, green pepper, onion and garlic until limp, about 5 minutes. Remove the vegetables and set aside. If there is no oil left in pan, add about 15 ml (1 tbsp) more. Add the almonds, and stir frequently until lightly browned. Add the Worcestershire and stir well. Set aside.

In a large saucepan, bring 900 ml (1½ pts) water to the boil. Add the salt, pepper, tomato, spring onion, parsley, sautéed vegetables and almonds and return to the boil. Add the rice, stir well and reduce the heat to very low, cover and cook until all the water is absorbed and rice is fluffy, 20 –25 minutes. Or, to avoid scorching, you may turn off the burner and let rice cook in its own steam heat for the last few minutes.

CORN MANQUE CHOUX

SERVES 3–4

INGREDIENTS

25 g (1 oz) butter
30 ml (2 tbsp) vegetable oil
225 g (8 oz) corn kernels (4–6 fresh ears)
½ onion, chopped
1 garlic clove, finely chopped
50 g (2 oz) spring onion, chopped
15 ml (1 tbsp) sugar
1.5 ml (¼ tsp) black pepper
2.5 ml (½ tsp) salt
1.5 ml (¼ tsp) cayenne
120 ml (4 fl oz) poultry stock (page 12) or canned chicken broth
15 ml (1 tbsp) butter
1 egg, lightly beaten
120 ml (4 fl oz) milk

In a frying pan over medium heat, melt 15 ml (1 tbsp) butter with the oil. Sauté the corn, onion, garlic and green pepper, stirring often, until the onion is limp and transparent, about 5 minutes. Add the seasonings, and stir until combined. Add the stock and reduce heat to very low and simmer until liquid has almost evaporated, stirring often. Stir in 15 ml (1 tbsp) butter until melted and mixed in.

In a small bowl, mix together the egg and milk, whisking until frothy. Add to the corn, stirring well, until the mixture is heated through.

SPICY GREEN BEANS

SERVES 3–4

INGREDIENTS

1 lb fresh green beans, topped and tailed
30 ml (2 tbsp) vegetable oil
30 ml (2 tbsp) white wine vinegar
15 ml (1 tbsp) fresh-squeezed lemon juice
5 ml (1 tsp) Creole mustard
1 garlic clove, finely chopped
1 spring onion, finely chopped
5 ml (1 tsp) red-pepper flakes
1.5 ml (¼ tsp) salt

Cook the green beans in boiling water until just tender, 3–4 minutes. Drain and plunge into cold water, then drain well again.

In glass or other non-reactive dish whisk together all the remaining ingredients. Add the beans and stir to coat thoroughly. Refrigerate at least 3 hours. Serve cold.

Ingredients

450 g (1 lb) dried kidney beans, picked over
30–60 ml (2–4 tbsp) vegetable oil or bacon drippings
450 g (1 lb) chopped onion
4 stalks celery, chopped
2½ green peppers, chopped
2 cloves garlic, finely chopped
225 g (8 oz) Tasso, cubed
225 g (8 oz) Andouille sausage, sliced
2 bay leaves
10 ml (2 tsp) salt
10 ml (2 tsp) ground cumin
5 ml (1 tsp) dry mustard
15 ml (1 tbsp) chopped fresh oregano or 1 tsp dried
1.5 ml (¼ tsp) black pepper
1.5 ml (¼ tsp) cayenne
225 g (8 oz) spring onion, chopped
1 stalk celery, chopped
½ green pepper, chopped
45 ml (3 tbsp) chopped fresh parsley
575–675 kg (1¼–1½ lb) cooked rice to serve

Red Beans and Rice with Tasso and Andouille

Makes 6–8 main course servings

In 4.5 l (1 gallon) water, soak the beans at least 4 hours or overnight. Drain, rinse and return to the large pot with 1.25 l (2¼ pts) water. Bring to the boil, then reduce the heat and simmer, skimming the foam, while you prepare the vegetables.

In the meanwhile, in a frying pan, heat the oil or drippings and sauté the 450 g (1 lb) onion, 4 chopped stalks celery, the chopped green peppers and 2 cloves garlic until wilted, about 5 minutes. Unless you use a very large frying pan, it is easier to sauté the vegetables in 2 batches. Add the vegetables to the beans, along with the Tasso, sausage and seasonings and continue simmering, stirring occasionally, until beans are tender, 1–1½ hours. Add extra water if necessary. Taste and adjust seasonings.

Just before serving, stir in the last measure of spring onions, celery, green pepper and parsley and mix well. Serve over rice.

Duck Rice

SERVES 4–6

Oven Temperature:
180°C/350°F/Gas Mark 4

In a frying pan over medium heat, heat the duck fat or oil. Sauté the onions and mushrooms until the onions are translucent, about 5 minutes. Add the rice and cook until it is lightly browned, about 5 minutes.

Meanwhile, in a saucepan, bring the duck stock, seasonings and celery leaves to the boil. Combine the rice and stock mixtures in a lightly greased 2 l (3½ pts) casserole dish and stir in the duck and spring onions. Cover and bake at 180°C/350°F/Gas Mark 4 until all the liquids are absorbed and rice is cooked, about 1 hour.

Ingredients

30 ml (2 tbsp) duck fat or vegetable oil
100 g (4 oz) chopped onions
50 g (2 oz) sliced mushrooms
350 g (12 oz) uncooked rice
750 ml (1¼ pts) duck stock
10 ml (2 tsp) salt
10 ml (2 tsp) fresh thyme or 2.5 ml (½ tsp) dried
10 ml (2 tsp) paprika
2.5 ml (½ tsp) black pepper
30 ml (2 tbsp) finely chopped celery leaves
100 g (4 oz) chopped spring onions
350 g (12 oz) cooked duck meat, cut into strips or bite-sized pieces

INGREDIENTS

50 g (2 oz) Parmesan cheese, grated
75 g (3 oz) cornmeal
5 ml (1 tsp) cayenne
5 ml (1 tsp) onion powder
5 ml (1 tsp) celery salt
2.5 ml (½ tsp) salt
2.5 ml (½ tsp) garlic powder
2 eggs, lightly beaten
120 ml (4 fl oz) milk
few drops of Tabasco sauce
1 large aubergine, cut into 5mm (¼-in) thick slices
vegetable oil for frying

DEEP-FRIED AUBERGINE

SERVES 5–4

In a bowl, combine the cheese, cornmeal and spices. In a second bowl, combine the eggs, milk and Tabasco sauce.

Dip the aubergine slices into the cornmeal a second time.

In a deep frying pan or wok, heat 5–7.5 cm (2–3in) of oil to 180°C/350°F. With tongs, gently drop 3–5 slices of aubergine into the oil, taking care not to crowd, and fry until golden brown on both sides, turning once, about 2 minutes a side. Drain briefly on kitchen paper and keep warm in the oven as you fry the aubergine. Ensure the oil returns to 180°C/350°F before frying the next batch.

Chapter Four

Chicken and Seafood

Chicken and Andouille Sausage Gumbo

■

Seafood Jambalaya

■

Blackened Redfish

■

Chicken, Andouille and Prawn Jambalaya

■

Crawfish Pie

■

Seafood Gumbo with Okra

■

Barbecued Shark

■

Crawfish Étouffée

■

Almond Trout

Chicken and Andouille Sausage Gumbo

SERVES 6

Mix 45 ml (3 tbsp) flour with the seasonings in a small bowl, then toss the chicken until the cubes are well coated with spices. Heat the oil in a large frying pan and sauté the chicken until browned. Drain on kitchen paper, if necessary. Set aside.

Combine the remaining flour and the lard to make a dark, mahogany-coloured roux (page 13). Remove the roux from the heat and add the chopped vegetables. Stir until the roux stops darkening. Return to the heat and cook until the vegetables are limp, about 5 minutes.

Add the poultry stock, a little at a time, stirring until well blended. Bring to the boil,then add the chicken, Andouille and garlic. Reduce the heat and simmer for 1 hour. You may wish to skim the gumbo occasionally if fat from the roux or the sausage rises to the top. Taste and adjust seasonings. Serve over rice.

Ingredients

25 g (1 oz) plain flour
5 ml (1 tsp) salt
2.5 ml (½ tsp) black pepper
1.5 ml (¼ tsp) cayenne
5 ml (1 tsp) paprika
2.5 ml (½ tsp) onion powder
2.5 ml (½ tsp) garlic powder
3 whole or 6 half uncooked chicken breasts, skinned and cubed
60 ml (2 fl oz) vegetable oil
100 g (4 oz) plain flour
225 g (8 oz) lard
450 g (1 lb) chopped onion
2 medium green peppers, chopped
3 stalks celery, chopped
1.75l (3¼ pts) poultry stock (page 12)
350 g (12 oz) Andouille sausage, cubed
2 garlic cloves, finely chopped
350 g (12 oz) cooked rice to serve

Seafood Jambalaya

SERVES 6–8

In a deep frying pan or Dutch oven, heat the oil. Sauté the onion, green pepper, celery and garlic until vegetables are limp, about 5 minutes. Add the tomatoes, tomato sauce, stock, parsley and seasonings and simmer gently until the tomatoes are cooked down and some of the liquids have reduced. Taste and adjust the seasonings.

Add the seafood. (If using oysters, cut into bite-sized pieces and add in last 2-3 minutes of cooking.) Simmer just until the prawns are opaque and tightly curled, 5–7 minutes. Just before serving, mix in the spring onions. Serve over rice.

NOTE:

If the rice is not cooked with salt, you will need additional salt in the jambalaya.

Ingredients

30 ml (2 tbsp) vegetable oil
1 onion, chopped
1 green pepper, chopped
2 stalks, celery, chopped
3 cloves garlic, finely chopped
3 large tomatoes, seeded and chopped
250 ml (8 fl oz) tin tomato sauce
250 ml (8 fl oz) seafood sauce (page 12)
50 g (2 oz) chopped fresh parsley
2 bay leaves
15 ml (1 tbsp) fresh thyme or 5 ml (1 tsp) dried
5 ml (1 tsp) salt
1.5 ml (¼ tsp) black pepper
2.5 ml (½ tsp) cayenne
large pinch white pepper
900 g (2 lbs) fresh prawns, crab meat, crawfish or oysters, or any combination, prepared
100 g (4 oz) spring onions, chopped
450 g (1 lb) cooked rice to serve

Ingredients

6 fish fillets

175 g (6 oz) unsalted butter, melted

Seasoning Mix

7.5 ml (1½ tsp) salt

15 ml (1 tbsp) paprika

5 ml (1 tsp) onion powder

5 ml (1 tsp) garlic powder

5 ml (1 tsp) dried thyme

2.5 ml (½ tsp) dried oregano

2.5 ml (½ tsp) black pepper

5 ml (1 tsp) cayenne

Butter Sauce

100 g (4 oz) unsalted butter, melted

15 ml (1 tbsp) fresh-squeezed lemon juice

1 spring onion, finely chopped

2.5 ml (¼ tsp) cayenne

2.5 ml (¼ tsp) salt

Blackened Redfish

SERVES 6

Put a cast-iron frying pan over high heat and heat until the pan begins to smoke and white ash forms on the bottom, at least 10 minutes. If after 20 minutes, there is no ash, your stove may not produce enough heat. Sprinkle a few drops of water in the pan. If they dance, the frying pan is hot enough to do the job, but cooking may take an extra 30 seconds a side.

Combine all the ingredients for the seasoning mix and set aside.

Combine all the ingredients for butter and set aside.

Dip the fillets in plain melted unsalted butter, then sprinkle the seasoning mix on both sides and pat into the butter. The butter will congeal on the cold fish and may flake off. If it does, put it in pan with the barest side up and spoon some melted butter over the bare spots. But be wary: the butter is likely to flame up during cooking. If it does, put a lid on the frying pan to smother the fire, then continue.

When the pan is ready, put 2 fillets in, moving quickly and cook until the bottoms are blackened, up to 2 minutes. (The fish will not be solid black, but ridges, edges and grains of seasonings will be blackened.) Turn over. If the thickness is not uniform, you may wish to press down gently with a spatula during cooking. Again, cook until ridges on bottom are blackened, up to 2 minutes. The interior of the fish should be opaque but juicy. Keep warm in a low oven while you repeat with the remaining fillets.

Reheat the butter sauce if necessary and pour over the fish. Serve at once.

Chicken, Andouille and Prawn Jambalaya

SERVES 6–8

Ingredients

5 ml (1 tsp) salt
2.5 ml (½ tsp) cayenne
2.5 ml (½ tsp black pepper
7.5 ml (1½ tsp) fresh or 2.5 ml (½ tsp) dried thyme
1 whole or 2 half uncooked chicken breasts, skinned and cubed
30 ml (2 tbsp) vegetable oil
3 stalks celery, chopped
2 medium onions, chopped
2 medium green peppers, chopped
2 garlic cloves, finely chopped
100 g (4 oz) Tasso or other smoked ham, chopped
150 g (6 oz) Andouille or other spicy sausage, sliced
450 g (1 lb) tomatoes, seeded and chopped
225-g (8-oz) tin tomato sauce
250 ml (8 fl oz) poultry or seafood stock (pages 12–13)
225 g (8 oz) medium shrimp, shelled and deveined
100 g (4 oz) spring onions, chopped
575 g (1¼ lb) cooked rice to serve

In a small bowl, mix together the salt, cayenne, black pepper and thyme. Toss the chicken, until it is well coated with spices.

In a large frying pan or Dutch oven, heat the oil. Sauté the chicken, stirring almost constantly, until the chicken is browned, 6–8 minutes. Add the celery, onion, green pepper and garlic, and sauté until the vegetables are limp, about 5 minutes.

Add the Tasso, Andouille sausage, tomatoes, tomato sauce and stock and stir and cook until mixture is bubbling. Reduce the heat and simmer until tomatoes have cooked down and liquid is slightly reduced, creating a rich, red broth. Add the prawns and cook until the prawns are opaque and tightly curled, 2–3 minutes. Taste and adjust the seasonings. It should be very spicy. Add the spring onions and enough rice so that the mixture is neither soupy nor dry.

NOTE:
If you did not cook the rice with salt, you will need to increase the amount of salt in the jambalaya.

CRAWFISH PIE

SERVES 6–8

In a heavy saucepan, make a peanut-butter-coloured roux of lard and flour (page 13). Remove from the heat, add the vegetables, garlic and parsley. Return to the heat, and cook until the vegetables are wilted, about 5 minutes.

In another pan, heat the seafood stock and single cream to a slow boil. Whisk in the roux, 1 large spoonful at a time, whisking after each addition. Add the seasonings and lemon juice and bring to the boil, then reduce the heat and simmer for 20 minutes. Add the crawfish tails and spring onions. Taste and adjust the seasonings, then let cool to lukewarm.

Roll out the piecrust dough and line a 23-cm (9-inch) pie tin with half the dough, sprinkling a little flour over the bottom to prevent sogginess. Add filling and top with the second crust. Trim and seal the edges, pinching into a fluted edge.

Bake at 190°C/375°F/Gas Mark 5 until the crust is golden brown, about 30 minutes. Let cool about 10 minutes before serving.

INGREDIENTS

50 g (2 oz) lard
25 g (1 oz) plain flour
100 g (4 oz) onion, chopped
1 large stalk celery, chopped
½ large green pepper, chopped
2 garlic cloves, finely chopped
30 ml (2 tbsp) chopped fresh parsley
120 ml (4 fl oz) seafood stock (page 12) or clam juice
350 ml (2 fl oz) single cream
5 ml (1 tsp) paprika
4 ml (¾ tsp) fresh thyme or ¼ tsp dried
7.5 ml (1½ tsp) chopped fresh basil or ½ tsp dried
1.5 ml (¼ tsp) black pepper
1.5 (¼ tsp) cayenne
large pinch white pepper
5 ml (1 tsp) salt
10 ml (2 tsp) fresh-squeezed lemon juice
675 g (1½ lbs) crawfish tails, shelled and cooked
6 spring onions, chopped
pastry dough for 2-crust pie

Ingredients

30 ml (2 tbsp) vegetable oil
450 g (1 lb) onions, chopped
2 large green peppers, chopped
2 stalks celery, chopped
3 garlic cloves, finely chopped
3 large or 4 medium tomatoes, seeded and chopped
250-g (8-oz) tin tomato sauce
1.75 l (3 pts) seafood stock (page 12)
15 ml (1 tbsp) fresh-squeezed lemon juice
2 bay leaves
15 ml (1 tbsp) fresh thyme or 5 ml (1 tsp) dried
5 ml (1 tsp) salt
1.5 ml (¼ tsp) black pepper
large pinch cayenne
large pinch white pepper
2.5 ml (½ tsp) paprika
675 g (1½ lbs) okra, thawed and well drained if frozen, sliced
900 ml (2 lbs) mixed seafood
450 g (1 lb) cooked rice to serve
filé powder, optional

Seafood Gumbo with Okra

SERVES 8

In a large frying pan, heat the oil. Sauté the onion, pepper, celery and garlic until limp, about 5 minutes. Transfer to a large saucepan or stockpot and add the tomatoes, tomato sauce, seafood stock, lemon juice and seasonings. Bring to the boil, then reduce the heat and simmer, uncovered, 5 minutes.

Add the okra and return to the boil, then reduce the heat and simmer 30 minutes. Add the seafood: cubed fish and frogs' legs take the longest times to cook, oysters the least.

Spoon the rice into individual large bowls. Ladle the gumbo over the rice. If desired, add a pinch of filé powder to each bowl.

BARBECUED SHARK

SERVES 4

In a glass or other non-reactive dish, combine all the ingredients, except the shark and pepper. Place the shark steaks in the marinade, turning to coat thoroughly, and spreading dill and garlic bits over tops of the fish. Sprinkle with fresh-ground black pepper, cover with cling film and refrigerate about 2 hours, turning once or twice.

When the barbecue coals have stopped flaming, place the shark steaks on a lightly greased grill. Cook about 5 minutes each side, turning once. (Total cooking time should be about 10 minutes per inch of thickness.) Baste with the extra marinade, if desired. The fish is cooked through when the flesh turns opaque, but is still juicy.

INGREDIENTS

45 ml (3 tbsp) fresh-squeezed lemon juice
45 ml (3 tbsp) fresh-squeezed lime juice
2.5 ml (½ tsp) grated lemon peel
2.5 ml (½ tsp) grated lime peel
60 ml (2 fl oz) olive oil
45 ml (3 tbsp) chopped fresh dill
3 garlic cloves, finely chopped
pinch of salt
4 shark steaks, about 175 g (6 oz) each
fresh-ground black pepper

Crawfish Étouffée

SERVES 4–6

Ingredients

100 g (4 oz) lard
50 g (2 oz) plain flour
225 g (8 oz) onion, chopped
1 large green pepper, chopped
1 large stalk celery, chopped
4 cloves garlic, finely chopped
4 medium tomatoes, seeded and chopped
75 g (3 oz) fresh parsley, chopped
475 ml (16 fl oz) seafood stock (page 12)
2.5 ml (½ tsp) cayenne
2.5 ml (½ tsp) black pepper
5ml (1 tsp) salt
7.5 ml (1½ tsp) black pepper
5 ml (1 tsp) salt
7.5 ml (1½ lbs) crawfish tails, shelled and cooked
8 spring onions, chopped
225–350 g (8–12 oz) cooked rice to serve

In a heavy saucepan, make a mahogany-coloured roux of the lard and flour (page 13.) Remove from the heat, stir in the vegetables and parsley. Return to the heat and cook until the vegetables are limp, about 5 minutes.

In large saucepan, bring the seafood stock to a slow boil. Add the roux and vegetables, 1 spoonful at a time, whisking after each addition until the mixture is smooth. Add the seasoning. Reduce the heat and simmer for 30 minutes.

Add the crawfish tails and simmer until crawfish is heated through, about 5 minutes. Just before serving, stir in the spring onions. Serve over rice.

ALMOND TROUT

SERVES 2

INGREDIENTS

2 small trout, about 450 g (1 lb) each, filleted with the heads removed (can be whole or in 2 pieces)
30 ml (2 tbsp) olive oil
2.5 ml (½ tsp) paprika
40 g (1½ oz) butter
75 g (3 oz) sliced blanched almonds
5 ml (1 tsp) Worcestershire sauce
10 ml (2 tsp) freshly-squeezed lemon juice
5 m, (1 tsp) grated lemon peel
few drops of Tabasco sauce
3 spring onions, chopped
30 ml (2 tbsp) chopped fresh parsley

Spray a grill pan with a non-stick spray. Put the trout on the rack, skin side down. Combine the olive oil and paprika, and brush over filleted meat. Put under the hot grill, about 5 inches from the heat, and grill unskinned side up until opaque but still juicy, 5–6 minutes, using a rule of 10 minutes per 2.5 (1 in) of the fillet's thickness.

While fish is cooking, in a small frying pan, melt the butter. Add the almonds and cook until they are a golden brown. Add the Worcestershire sauce, lemon juice, lemon peel and Tabasco sauce and mix well. Remove from the heat, add the spring onions and parsley, and quickly spoon over the grilled trout.